THE COMPOSER'S ASSISTANT'S HANDBOOK

The Things They Don't Tell You

JAIKUMAR SIVALINGAM

Copyright © 2020
Jaikumar Sivalingam
The Composer's Assistant's Handbook
The Things They Don't Tell You
All rights reserved.

No part of this publication may be reproduced, distributed, or transmitted in any form or by any means, including photocopying, recording, or other electronic or mechanical methods, without the prior written permission of the publisher, except in the case of brief quotations embodied in critical reviews and certain other non-commercial uses permitted by copyright law.

Jaikumar Sivalingam

Printed in the United States of America
First Printing 2020
First Edition 2020

10 9 8 7 6 5 4 3 2 1

The Composer's Assistant's Handbook

TABLE OF CONTENTS

Chapter 1 1

Why I'm Writing This Book

Chapter 2 7

Intern vs Composer's Assistant

Chapter 3 15

Skills Required for a Composer's Assistant

Chapter 4 21

Where to Look for Composer's Assistant Jobs

Chapter 5 25

What Keeps Modern Composers Broke

Chapter 6 29

The Things They Don't Tell You

Chapter 7 61

Tools & Resources

Chapter 8 67

Acknowledgements

Chapter 1

Why I'm Writing This Book

My Foray into Music Production

From 2008 to 2012, I was working as an IT employee in India. The work was extremely stressful, with long working hours (16 to 18 hrs) and low pay, and I kept falling sick. I wanted to explore other options, and when doing so, I came to know about music production. I was good at and loved both technology and music, so I quit my job and plunged head first into music production. Of course, with the customary opposition and 'have you gone mad?!' comments from family and well wishers.

I didn't want to learn outdated techniques through a random university degree. So I found someone whose work was extraordinary and who was active in the industry – Mr Hentry Kuruvila, one of the orchestrators and music producers for the Oscar winner AR Rahman. In Jan 2013, I joined Hentry's Musikport in Chennai, India and pursued a diploma in music technology.

Days as an Intern

Soon after completing the course, I got to work as an audio engineering intern at one of the popular studios in Mumbai. Mumbai, the city of dreams, has blessed me immensely since 2013. Transitioning from working in an IT desk job to a studio gave me goosebumps. I had some amazing opportunities to meet a lot of talents, and I got to learn how recordings were done professionally at a studio. Until then, I had learnt things alone with a home studio setup, so initially, I felt very nervous. All my life, I'd been an introvert, but suddenly, I was in a studio, meeting strangers, recording background vocals with singers and voice actors I used to admire, and recording instruments. The work was very challenging because speed mattered. I am so grateful to Groove3.com, macprovideo.com, and the Youtube channels Recording Revolution and Pensado's Place which helped me to learn things quicker. I was lucky enough that my boss gave me the studio keys, and I made sure that I always spent extra hours practicing pro tools and routing audio through different analog gears effectively using patchbay.

As days went by, cleaning the tracks with strip silence, drawing fades to the new tracks, prepping the session, and keeping the tracks ready for the mix became the only tasks. Some music producers even asked me why I was wasting time drawing only fades when I had a background in music; I could rather donate sperms and make more money, they said!

Eventually, after a month, like Gary Keller says in his book *The One Thing*, I started to question myself if I was at the right place. Are the things that I am doing today linked to my 5-year plan? When my answer was a No, even though I was getting paid – though a pittance it was, I moved out of the studio and began looking for a job as a composer's assistant. Because, I wanted to be a composer, not an engineer.

Days as a Composer's Assistant

I came back to Chennai as I got an opportunity to work with the composer Pradeep Kumar in one of his Telugu projects. I spent most of my time job shadowing, which is an effective way to know how a composer scores musical cues for a film. I learnt the importance of job shadowing from composer John Stewart Eduri who was kind enough to let me watch his process of orchestral layering during one of his MIDI mockup sessions for the film *Roar* (I am grateful for that, John!).

When assisting Pradeep, I got an opportunity to learn how he recorded a string quartet from Boston with students of Berklee College of Music. It was fascinating to watch and learn how the recordings served the picture. Also, I was given the opportunity to score two scenes; they were approved by the production team and ended up in the film. This was the eureka moment for me. When the project was just wrapping up, I got another opportunity to work with composer Radhan on a Tamil film project. On completion, I went on to score many short films by approaching students and budding directors who were a part of the reality show Naalaya Iyakunar Season 05. One of the short films I scored, *Meera*, won the award for the best film score. This gave me confidence, for I realised that film scores are nothing but a collection of multiple musical cues!

I went back to Mumbai in 2015, and within a couple of days, I was asked to ghost-write and score a Bollywood indie film. The score went on to receive a Certificate of Excellence in the background music category in the 6th Dada Saheb Phalke Film Festival, 2016, in Delhi. By networking and meeting a lot of composers, being their assistant, and ghost-writing music for them, I built a showreel that landed me in a gig as a music composer for one of the prominent shows on Disney Kids – Eena Meena Deeka; it was streamed in 7 countries. This landed me in another project for Turner's – Roll No 21 (Hoola Boola). Then Turner led me to many others…

Why I'm Writing This Book

From being a music student → composer's assistant → and then becoming a composer, every composer's journey is very unique. However, I had this feeling that I wish somebody had given me a road map which could have saved me from a lot of situations that were nowhere near nice! It has taken me 11 years to learn the key aspects of the business of media composition with the help of Google, Youtube, podcasts, taking private lessons, and most importantly, by being in the field and constantly learning from the music fraternity. The contents of this book are hence born from learning, interpreting, and transforming the methods of many truly gifted peers and mentors to model a system that is efficient for me. That is why Chapter 6 – The Things They Don't Tell You – is longer than the rest!

Like many writers, I too fear what the world would think of me when I share my experiences through this book. But I'm doing it anyway because I believe that it will help you wade through the storms and calms in your own voyage through this grand sea of music, and I sincerely hope that it will bring you immense success, peace, and happiness.

Chapter 2

Intern vs Composer's Assistant

Why be an Intern or a Composer's Assistant When You Can Directly Become a Composer?

Music schools and universities, books, or blogs will neither be able to give you an in depth experience that you will gain while actually scoring a picture, TV series, or games nor teach you the film scoring business. Hence it's important to learn from someone who has been doing it successfully.

You can develop your skill by shadowing/quietly observing the composer when he/she is working. By simply sitting next to a composer and observing how he/she works, one can get to know why/how an instrument is sampled or a sample library is chosen to get a particular sound, layering sounds, time-codes, and scoring scenes in different genres. Spending time as a composer's assistant will give you the kind of knowledge that you would get nowhere else.

Who is an Intern?

Composers/studios look for interns when they need someone to do generalized tasks. Hence, they usually hire students in the final year of their degree/course.

Skills Expected Out of an Intern

- Good command over at least one Digital Audio Workstation (DAW)
- Ability to listen to and communicate well
- Ability to adapt to the studio environment
- Open to learn on the job

What Interns Do?

The daily activities of an intern includes, but not limited to:

- Fetching coffee and food
- Opening and locking the studio everyday
- Keeping the composer's desk and studio clean
- Running around to receive new files, documents, cheques, etc.

- Assisting the engineer or composer during recording sessions
- Receiving clients when a composer is in another room, finishing up unexpected tasks
- Cable management
- Performing MIDI mockups
- Troubleshooting gears

Types of Internships

1. Paid - You'll get a monthly salary

2. Unpaid - It's very common in India; you'll be given free lunch coupons, if you are lucky that is!

Who is a Composer's Assistant?

Due to the amazing real time performance and technical advancements in Solid State Drives (SSD) and computers, composers more often than not have tight deadlines. However, the same have led to a laborious scoring process and most composers find it challenging to deliver the score on time without a team. A composer's assistant is an important member of this team who shares the load of the composer.

What Composer's Assistants Do?

The below is the list of tasks expected out of a composer's assistant:

- Simple tech tasks like formatting HDDs, SSDs, computer machines, etc.
- Installing Kontakt and other sample libraries
- Setting up networking - master-slave (disciple) systems, troubleshooting
- Taking notes in meetings or spotting sessions
- Invoicing
- Organizational tasks like file renaming, copying, data backup, etc.
- Editing audio - pitch corrections, cleaning up, strip silence, etc.
- Realigning or syncing cues with new video edits
- Creating tempo maps and recording click tracks as a separate wave file
- Ensuring that all gears in the studio are up and running smoothly
- Preparing recording sessions
- Creating templates from the existing sessions
- Converting MIDI into audio
- Preparing stems (strings, brass, winds, etc.)

Types of Composer's Assistants

1. Do-everything assistant
2. Ghostwriter
3. MIDI programmer
4. Studio technician
5. Personal assistant

1. <u>Do-everything assistant:</u> supports the composer in almost everything he/she does such as composing, arranging, additional programming, creating templates out of existing cues from a project, audio editing, pitch correcting and prepping the session for a recording, score preparation, mixing, cleaning up the MIDI, bouncing and delivering stems, and invoicing

2. <u>Ghostwriter:</u> may work in the composer's studio or remotely with a composer; after signing a NDA (Non-disclosure agreement), he composes, orchestrates, and/or scores multiple cues required for a project. Ghostwriters are paid a huge sum of money with no credits or royalty shares

3. <u>MIDI programmer:</u> composes or arranges and develops multiple cues for a composer with the help of virtual instruments. MIDI programmers are in huge demand for their realistic mockups

4. <u>Studio technician:</u> keeps the studio up and running and ensures that all the gears in the studio are patched and work well with a patch bay. Studio technicians are well-versed in MIDI connectivity programs, like Vienna Ensemble Pro which helps composers to host all their sample libraries on separate machines *(slaves/disciples)* and are responsible for organising Digital Audio Workstation (DAW) templates on the main master machine

5. <u>Personal assistant:</u> takes care of administrative tasks such as scheduling appointments and meetings, answering emails, maintaining websites, handling social media posts, ordering food, ordering equipment/gears, booking flight tickets, accounting, invoicing, preparing cheques, etc.

How to Know When to Self-promote from an Intern to a Composer's Assistant?

As you spend time in the studio or with the composer, you would get to know how a studio/composer functions. In your free time, reach out to film students and ask them if you could score their short films. As you keep working on student projects, you would gain confidence; besides developing an effective composing process, you would also have a good showreel. You could then share your showreel with the composer you are working for, and when the time is right, you could request if they would allow you to score a cue. Over a period of time, by taking feedback and working closely with the composer, there would come a point when you will have the confidence that you can deliver the kind of output a composer would want. This is when you can self-promote yourself from an intern to a composer's assistant and begin to look for composer's assistant jobs.

You might have heard this story: *Game of Thrones* composer Ramin Djawadi used to be an intern and used to make coffee for Hans Zimmer at *Remote*

Control Productions. One night, Hans couldn't get a cue right, so he decided to head home, leaving the work for the next day. Ramin requested Hans if he could work on it; Hans agreed, not expecting anything to come out of it. But when Hans came back in the morning and played Ramin's cue, he was surprised that it fit the scene perfectly.

He had happily told Ramin, 'You've fixed the missing piece in the cue now, and I'll see to that you never make coffee again!' As the story proves, an intern may later become a composer's assistant (and eventually, a composer) if they are a problem solver!

Chapter 3

Skills Required for a Composer's Assistant

Technical Skills

<u>Good hands-on experience with the DAW that the composer is using:</u> A composer may not be using your favourite DAW, so it's important that you have the willingness to learn a new DAW and adapt to the composer's workflows. I am a Logic Pro user, but when I began to work with Lesle Lewis, I had to learn Pro Tools as that was the DAW he used. With the help of the video tutorials from groove3.com and macprovideo.com, I familiarialised myself with Pro Tools.

<u>Good with advanced MIDI orchestrations:</u> It's extremely important to know the advanced MIDI functionalities within the DAW so that with the help of MIDI CC1 (modulation) and CC11 (expression), sample libraries could be leveraged to sound as realistic as possible. The expression maps in Cubase

Pro is a great feature which lets you mockup a piece without having to instantiate new tracks for additional articulations such as staccato, pizzicato, etc. If you are using the composer's machine for MIDI mockups, ensuring that you replace the key commands that you are using with the existing ones that the composer uses will save you from getting fired!

<u>Good with music preparation softwares:</u> Being an expert with music preparation softwares, like Sibelius and Finale, helps composer's assistants to record orchestra. Tristan Noon's *From DAW to Score* is a great eBook that could be your comprehensive guide for this.

<u>Ability to turn ideas into music:</u> Many a time, you might get an opportunity to work and communicate with production studios directly and play the role of the composer. It is common to be given an existing piece of music (which is also called temp tracks) as a reference. You would have to understand and develop an ear for what the production studio actually wants – is it the mood, tempo, or instrumentation of the temp track – and deliver cues accordingly.

<u>Preparing templates with Vienna Ensemble Pro:</u> Many composers like to have huge templates and have their samples installed on a separate (slave or disciple) machine. Vienna Ensemble Pro is a network hosting application that enables one to set up multiple computer networks with both mac and PCs, with a simple ethernet cable. It's essential for a composer's assistant to have a deep knowledge about preparing templates with Vienna Ensemble Pro.

<u>Assist the engineer or composer during recording sessions:</u> As a composer's assistant, you might be asked to record vocalists or instrumentalists in the absence of the composer. So it's important that you develop a good ear and skills to record and capture enough clean, good takes with the actual and variations and to name them correctly for the composer to choose from to complete a cue.

<u>Problem solving:</u> It's not advisable for a composer's assistant to call the composer as soon as a computer crashes or a program fails. Remember that you are a problem solver and try to troubleshoot and get it solved, unless it's a hardware failure.

<u>Score mixing:</u> When you are asked to do a mockup, you can't fix a cue if it had been poorly arranged during the mix; a good mix comes from a good arrangement. So a composer's assistant must be a good arranger besides having good mixing skills.

<u>Preparing cue sheets:</u> On completion of the scoring for a project, you could be asked to prepare its cue sheets from the spotting notes.

While preparing the cue sheets, it's good to remember to include the entire length of the reverb tails in the cues. CueDB is a great web application which can be used for this process, from spotting to submitting cue sheets.

<u>Google Docs/Microsoft Office:</u> Occasionally, you might be dealing with administrative tasks or handling emails and documents.

So it's good to have basic skills in Google Docs or MS Office.

Interpersonal Skills

As composers/composer's assistants, we would be working with different types of people from different backgrounds. Hence it's important for us to be easy to work with, have zero ego, communicate effectively, and have a good relationship with peers. Always remember that we are here to serve the picture, not to prove or justify our perspectives, even when we are right, especially when we are right.

Social Skills

Always carry an attitude of being professional, fun to work with, extremely reliable, and trustworthy. As a precaution, never gossip or email about any producer, film maker, composers, or other film crew members within or outside the studio because some way or the other, the news would spread and people will remember names, including yours!

You might get invited to parties, film premieres, award ceremonies, and trailer launches. These are the places you would most likely meet your idols (and by now, you would have realised that they are only your potential collaborators).

Go talk to them and tell them how their music/film/book inspired you; they would feel good about it when it's genuine. Never trouble them for selfies if they are talking with a group of people or if you see them spending time with their family.

Be genuinely interested when having a conversation with someone, and don't prepare your next question in your mind without listening, for the person who is talking to you might sense it and soon, he/she might walk away. Unless they ask for your visiting card, never take it out and force it on them; it creates a very bad first impression.

Chapter 4

Where to Look for Composer's Assistant Jobs

Before applying for a composer's assistant job, make sure you have a presentable showreel. If you feel that the music you created years ago sounds shitty, please do exclude it from the showreel. Your showreel doesn't have to be flooded with 100 tracks. It could simply be even one amazing track. Use the power of social media to promote that one good track you have and to position yourself properly.

Many studios and composers get in touch with colleges and ask for those who might be interested in being interns/composer's assistants. If you, like me, have not been to a music college, then look out for job openings on Craigslists, Indeed, Facebook Groups, Instagram posts, and Linkedin posts. If you are prepared enough, eventually an opportunity will present itself. Meet people in industry networking events such as film festivals, music workshops, [Palm Expo](), [NAMM](), [PAX](), [GDC](), [G.A.N.G]() etc.

Take help from friends and get passes to attend film premieres that happen in your locality. Go to house parties where your friends can introduce you to other composers.

I have tried all the above methods. I still do, and though old school, often, they work. But what has also worked fabulously for me is cold emailing to set up appointments and meet composers.

A Bit about Cold Emailing

<u>Identify your target composers:</u> Go to IMDb.com and search for the films that have your favourite music. Check who the composers are – they are your potential prospects. Look up their projects; their future projects would be tagged as post-production in their respective pages.

<u>Connect via social media:</u> Check if the composer is available on Facebook or LinkedIn and look for their email id/website and get in touch with them. I want to thank Daniel Ciurlizza, the founder of Outlier Studios, for the cold email template he has made available. I have modified it to suit me; please find it below.

Example emailing script:

Hello *(name of the composer),*

I'm *(your name).* I love your *(name unique stuff — orchestration, sound design, choice of instruments)* work on *(name of the project).* I got to know from IMDb that you are working on the *(name of the project).* Congratulations!

Do you have a requirement for a composer's assistant? If so, I would love to be your assistant and learn from you. Please find my profile/resume attached *(attach a well-written resume in pdf format)* and my showreel here *(add the link to your presentable showreel).*

May I call you on *(dd/mm/yyyy)* at *(time)* to discuss?

Warm regards,

Your name

(Your mobile number & Website)

If you don't hear from them immediately, have patience; they may be receiving thousands of emails every day. But make sure you follow-up with the composer. More on the follow-up etiquettes will be discussed in Chapter 6.

Most importantly, never attach multiple wav/video files directly to the email as it would clutter and sometimes even collapse the composer's email storage, making sure that he/she might not reply to you at all!

Chapter 5

What Keeps Modern Composers Broke

There's this quote that I read somewhere on Instagram: 'Teach someone music product-ion and they'll never be rich again!'

One of the things that is keeping the modern audio enthusiasts broke is the gear acquisition syndrome. The belief that good – read expensive – gears are essential to create good music is simply a myth. You don't have to spend every penny you earn to update or keep buying every plugin, mics, or monitors that are being released everyday unless you have a project demand and unless it's a paid project. If your existing gears meet a project's requirements, then continue to make use of your existing gears and virtual instruments for the project. Also, buying on Black Friday/spring sales saves money. When we pay for a plugin, we tend to respect it more than pirated softwares.

Rent a studio whenever it's possible. Over the years, I have figured out that by renting studios, I am able to use outboard gears and experiment with them. Save up to invest wisely on gears. Unfortunately, over a period of time, all gears depreciate in value. So don't overspend by using credit cards and end up in debt.

Some people simply collect every crack – pirated plugins and virtual instruments – just like adding random people as friends on Facebook! Just because Neve 88 RS console is priceless (pun intended), it cannot turn crappy music into good music. Instead, if you master the original gears and stock plugins that you already have and squeeze the maximum out of them, it will help keep your wallet filled with dollars.

Every time I meet beginners, they ask me what gears to use. So here is a list of gears that I recommend for a professional composer. You don't have to buy everything in this list at once, and needless to say, this is not the ultimate gears list per se. Upgrades can be incremental over a period of time.

Home Studio - 2020 - Gear Recommendation		
Studio Acoustics/Room Correction		
Acoustic Panels	Primacoustic London 12	1
Desk	OutPut - Platform/Hire a carpenter - custom desk	1
Chair	A height-adjustable chair (doesn't have to be an Aeron Miller!)	1
Calibration Kit	Sonarworks Reference 4 with mic	1
Digital Audio Workstation		
Reaper or Logic Pro X		
Machine		
Master 01	Macbook Pro 15" 64GB / Mac mini 2018 - 128GB	1
Display		
Screen 01	24" LED screen	1
Connectivity		
Dock	HyperDrive TUBE 6-in-1 USB-C Hub	1

Audio		
Audio Interface	Focusrite scarlett	1
Headphones	Beyerdynamic 990 Pro	1
Audio Monitors	JBL 305P MkII 5" or 8"	2
Audio Monitor Mount	Isoacoustics - ISO155-isolation-stands	2
MIDI Controllers		
Controller	Komplete A – 61	1
Storage		
Samples/Video Write	Samsung EVO 860 (get enclosures)	2
Onsite Backup Software	Carbon Copy Cloner	1
Backup Solution		
Remote Backup	Google Drive	1

Chapter 6

The Things They Don't Tell You

Culture Shock

If you are moving to a different city, be prepared to experience culture shock. It's easy to get carried away by judging people and de-motivate yourself. Taking a non-egoistic approach and remembering why you moved to that city in the first place will keep your eyes on your goal.

Stick to the 5-year Plan

If you are keen to work in Hollywood, then you definitely have to live in Hollywood. Move into the city that is the hub of your work and give it 5 years to really see the results. The general myth that it takes 5 years (or 10,000 hours) for a beginner to make it in a new city is not a myth at all; it is true! I began working out of Mumbai from March 2015, and I have just finished my five years in Bollywood.

You might not land on your dream job on Day 1. But don't get disappointed and think a hundred times and more before deciding to quit the industry or to move out of the city you live and work in. When I was new to Mumbai, I met a producer at a friend's party. Then I followed up with him occasionally for 6 months before he called me to score for a Disney animated series. That was my first gig as a composer. That gig helped me get another animated series for Tuner after a year. It is a chain reaction. One job lands you into another. So everything you do after moving to a new city matters! And your career might look like this: Scoring student films → Shorts → Documentaries → Indie Films → TV Series → Medium budget film → High budget films. Or if you are lucky, it could be High budget films → Oscar! Whatever the route is, have patience and network consistently while also simultaneously building an amazing showreel.

Working for Someone You Admire

If you are just out of college with a degree in film music and a huge student debt because of the high tuition fees and the purchase of the mandatory sample libraries, MacBook pro, DAW, and plugins, you might be one of the many new composers who are under financial pressure. Due to this, a lot of new composers try to find assistant jobs that involve a contract (where you cannot freelance for anyone else) for the next couple of years. This could become a toxic environment – not getting paid on time, the composer not picking up your calls whenever you try to reach them, and the composer regularly using abusive conduct or language in a way that makes you feel uncomfortable.

Such composers make the assistants feel trapped. This feeling becomes more intense for assistants from out of that town who have no friends or family who can support them. So the assistants still continue to work for such composers to meet their survival necessities, leading to depression over a period of time.

Don't let them break your confidence. Understand that you have come a very long way, be courageous, quit that place, and avoid the morons! Work with someone you admire to ensure that your passion remains as passion and doesn't become a tedious job. So when you look for composers to gain experience as an assistant, ensure that they are a good human with values that match yours.

Having a unique showreel would create an opportunity to work with people you admire. Besides, while working with another composer, never stop creating your own music. Block time for your passion projects, even if it means waking up early to work on them.

Avoiding Morons = Avoiding Burnouts

There are clients and composers who get you to work on a new video edit all night for an 'urgent' delivery and then forget to pay you. You would then have to follow up with them for days or even months for your payments. Incidentally, they are the same people who don't bother to give credits for your work. I've learnt it the hard way – please respect yourself and your health first. Give time to your family, to yourself, and to your health. You never opted for a career in music to only die from burnouts. Work with people who respect your time and efforts genuinely. If you don't respect yourself, nobody else will. The answer to every client's questions cannot always be a YES. Learn to say NO and understand this: no one, except yourself, can make you do what you don't want to do!

Keeping Your Calm – Meditate, Take Breaks, and Go for Walks

Take care of your body, meditate, get enough sleep, and take breaks. Since we are sitting for longer hours, the standing desks are becoming very popular. Use the Pomodoro technique to take breaks – the technique uses a timer to break down work into intervals, traditionally 25 minutes in length, separated by short breaks. After a few sessions, take a longer break. During the break, I usually go get a glass of water and stretch. Then I set the timer again and get back to work. I'm a fan of Focus, an app for android that lets a visual plant grow on your screen so you can see the time ticking. Block calendars for vacations. Give yourself breaks on the weekend or just about any two days in a week and let your body energise to perform well the following week.

To a new composer, this might sound like a yoga guru's advice! And it is easy to get caught up in a lifestyle of what seems to be the norm in the industry – long working hours, skipping food and surviving on coffee, little or no sleep, and no breaks and holidays. It might even feel cool to be telling yourself and others that you hardly have time for anything other than work. But if you take your wellbeing for granted, you would soon come to realise that you simply cannot make good music when you are sick.

The Money Game

Failing to plan financially might lead you to debts. Being in this business for a while will acclimatise you to big figure cheques; expecting the payment of an upcoming/ongoing project, you might be tempted to invest in gears that seem essential for your projects. If you do that but the project payment gets delayed or cancelled for whatever reasons, you might be in big trouble. Making use of credit cards for purchasing gears unnecessarily screws your credit score if your payments don't arrive on time. Always try to set up a template and save enough money to avoid living off the edges! I use the below template, for which I got the idea from Philip Olson and Julia Lorenz Olson (Two Cents). When you begin to get a steady cash flow, invest wisely in real estate, stocks, and bonds that pay you dividends and generate passive incomes; then you could invest on gears perhaps.

Like Dan Graham says in his book *A Composer's Guide to Library Music*, writing tracks for TV libraries brings you more money in the form of royalties. Get registered with BMI or ASCAP to be able to receive your unique IPI CAE number for receiving your royalty cheques or ACH.

Money Game – Template			
Segments	**Itineraries**	**Percentage**	**Bank**
Essentials	Rent & Electricity	14.40%	A
	Travel	5.00%	
	Food & Groceries	15.00%	
	Internet + Phone	2.00%	
	Credit Card – Optional		
	Send money to Family	4.00%	B
	Charity	1.00%	
Security	Emergency Funds	15.00%	C
	Paying Off Debts	22.49%	
	Baby	5.00%	
	Retirement Fund	1.11%	D
Goals	Business	1.00%	E
	Vacation	2.00%	

	House	2.00%	
Lifestyle	Personal Grooming	2.00%	F
	Gym Membership / Yoga / Swimming	2.00%	
	Books / Gifts for friends and family	1.00%	
Discretionary	Massage	2.00%	G
	Movie	2.00%	
	Dinner	1.00%	

In case you are not using any particular segment, then the money allotted to that segment has to be put into any one of the other segments.

Failing to Give Your 100% to Your Pitch

Here is an interesting perspective: 'Offered a chance to audition musical ideas for Captain Marvel, Pinar Toprak pulled out all the stops,' says an article in *Variety*. 'She composed about seven minutes of music and hired a 70-piece orchestra in L.A. to perform it. Then she created a short video of herself in her studio explaining her ideas. She won over directors Boden and Fleck and got the job.' I'm not asking you to malnourish your wallet every time you pitch for a project, but just remember that Pinar Toprak got the job because she gave her 100% when she pitched for Captain Marvel.

Failing to Understand What the Story Demands

Like James Horner explains in his famous TED talk, 'Writing music for film is very proprietary.' In simple English, it means that the music that you have been commissioned to write is owned by somebody else and you simply cannot incorporate anything without the approval of the producer, director, or the film company. After all, we – like many other craftsmen – are working for somebody else. More often than not, we may not share the same musical taste with our clients. During presentations, you might think that you just played astounding cues to your clients, but you might be given that look of pity and be asked to change the cues, sometimes even completely. No matter what you do, please never get into an argument! Nobody is interested in your counterpoint writing skill in that moment – so avoid being labelled a musical racist and take feedback constructively! After all, we are there to collectively serve the picture.

Never Release Your Music before You Get Paid

(I wish I could write this title in Bold, but my editor said a strong No!)

On project completion, please use a service like filepass.com which lets your clients pay and download your music; remember to mention this in your contract. Never release your music before getting paid. If you release it and then the studio doesn't pay for it, cry or break a glass or two to vent if need be, but don't ever plan on getting into lawsuits because besides the humongous cost, it's just pointless.

What Next?

In the past, I have spent more time thinking about the next step without paying enough attention to the one I was in. Obviously, I consider it crucial to have goals and planning, but as a guide, not an obsession. In high school, it was all about getting into a good college; in college, it was all about becoming a film composer; when I was scoring short films, it was all about getting my first feature, and so on. But scoring short films should be all about doing a great job scoring short films. Scoring a feature should be all about doing a great job scoring that feature, not about how to leverage it for the next one. Making the most of the present moment is worth contemplation, and it will naturally lead to the best next step.

80/20 Principle

The 80/20 or the Pareto principle states that for many events, roughly 80% of the effects come from 20% of the causes. For instance, though creating a website is very easy in WordPress, Wix, or Squarespace, you can find a good web designer on Fiverr for $30 to do it and spend that time creating a cue for a TV music library which could fetch you ($100 + royalties).

So only focus on the tasks that you are good at and don't hesitate to hire help or delegate any other tasks.

Be Clear about Your Contracts

Before starting a project, make a contract and always ensure that there is some kind of transaction involved. If you are not getting paid for the project, tell the production team that the tracks' music rights are non-exclusive and sell it multiple times on different licensing platforms or to multiple clients, generating multiple revenues from the tracks. Your future credibility starts with credits, so make sure that you get credits for the work you do. In the absence of contracts, use deal memos, which are informal contracts. There are so many deal memo templates available for free on Google. Also, it is best to avoid signing documents written in languages you don't understand. Heaven knows what is written in even documents that are in English!

Develop an Individual Style

It is awesome to be able to emulate another composer's music styles. But as a composer, block your time and guard it to develop your skills; get better at writing and cultivate an individual style. Composer Philip Glass liked writing music in a way he liked which later became his style and is widely recognised as good music. Having a unique style sets you apart from other competitors. It doesn't happen overnight, and it might take years. Like Fargo's composer Jeff Russo says, 'No one in the beginning of their career knows what they sound like. And if they tell you they know what they sound like, they are simply wrong.'

Create Custom Libraries for Projects

Get away from the sounds that are overused. Don't expect your music to stand out if you only use the overly used sample libraries that are available to every composer. Spend time on creating custom libraries to bring out a sonically unique story telling. By being able to use a sampler effectively to record, edit, and sample exotic instruments, one can add personality to their score and do the unexpected.

The Power of Collaboration

As composers, even when having a strong performing music background and touring with multiple bands, it's still difficult to master more than a genre. So it's essential to use the power of collaboration and know what your weaknesses are and seek out help from other composers and performing artists when the project demands so.

Even Hans Zimmer develops a unique style for almost every one of his projects by collaborating with other artists. In Gladiator, Hans has added mournful vocals of Lisa Gerrard. In Sherlock Holmes, he has worked with Gypsy musicians and has used unusual instruments. For Inception, Hans has collaborated with Johnny Marr who played the guitar parts in the score. Regardless of the genre, the style of music, or any other factor, adding a unique element to each score using the power of collaboration helps your music stand out among that of the competition!

Learn Screenwriting and Filmmaking

As John Powell explains in his master class, 'It's important to learn screenwriting and filmmaking if you are serious about film scoring.' Because you simply cannot write for a medium if you don't understand the medium. By understanding the medium, you can deliver and fulfil your directors' needs. Director Ridley Scott puts it across well: 'I listen to [Zimmer's] music and I don't even have to shut my eyes. I can see the pictures. And that's why, in many respects, I know I can talk pictures with Hans. He responds to pictures.'

Expanding Musical Capabilities

If you do not keep learning and expanding your musical sensibilities, your music might only reflect the music that you have heard since childhood. As composers, you could be writing a classical quartet cue today and an electronic ambient cue for a modern sci-fi film the next day. So keep expanding your musical capabilities to avoid sounding outdated.

Don't be a Victim of Shallow Learning

As composers or audio enthusiasts, we feel a rush of dopamine when we explore a new course online and as we complete it, we feel a sense of accomplishment. But if we don't apply what we learn, in addition to spending so much time on it, we will remain where we were before learning it.

This is the ultimate truth, but it could be overcome very easily – until you apply what you have learnt in a course, never binge watch another course or a tutorial on YouTube.

Instead, train your muscle memory with what you learnt until it becomes second nature.

Incorporate Form - ABA/AAA

By only listening to film music, you can learn a lot about melody, accompaniment, orchestration, themes, etc., but what you might not get is its proper FORM. That's because, film music is written to picture! So even if it makes no sense to repeat your melody four times for a piece of music, it might be exactly what's right when matched to the picture. And especially the ABA idea, which is central to so much instrumental music, becomes pointless when a villain pops up on screen and changes the dynamic entirely. So when it comes to form and structure and developing ideas, study music in the film's album /soundtrack. This means you focus on the classical, concert, and chamber works, or Main Titles or End Titles cues, but not the underscore that has been cut to match the picture.

Spatialisation - Rule of 3

While writing music, establish the foreground, middleground and background. Just like we use punctuations for writing, it's important to incorporate dynamics and spatialisation into music. The tone, articulations, chord voicing, and space add more three dimensional depth to the music. Also, sketching out the entire cue first and then orchestrating keeps you productive and helps in meeting the deadlines.

Make Your Project/Cue Names Unique

a. Naming Convention for Movie Cues

ProjectTitle_ReelNoMusicNo_CueName_VersionNo_YourInitials_FilmEditNo_SMPTE

ProjectTitle is the name of the client or the project, or it could be the actual title of the film; eg: BollywoodDiaries or BD (its acronym)

ReelNoMusicNo is the reel number of the film; eg: r01m01 would imply reel no 1, music no 1, r01m01b would imply its 2nd revision

CueName is the name of the cue; eg: Vanessa; for main titles, just keep the title of the track

VersionNo is the version number for the cue. Every time you make changes to a cue, it gets a new revised version number; eg: v1, v2, v3, and so on

YourInitials is, obviously, your initials; eg: JS for Jaikumar Sivalingam

FilmEditNo is the film edit number; eg: 0100

SMPTE denotes the timecode; eg 02032400 would be 02Hours:03Minutes:24Seconds:00Frames; even if my cue starts only at 02:03:24:21, I export the cue from 02032400, so that it's easier for the show runner and mixer at the dubstage to sync it to the picture

So the naming syntax goes like:

BD_r01m01_Vanessa_v1.0_JS_0100_02032400

b.　Naming Convention for TV Show Cues

ShowInitials(NoSpace)EpisodeNo-CueNo_CueName_VersionNo_FilmEditNo_SMPTE

Eg:RN004-7_HelpingJohn_v1.0_0100_01195321. For revised cues, indicate the revision number using alphabets; eg 27A, 27B, etc.

It's very simple, and the more you do it, the more it becomes instinctive, without requiring any thought. But it makes a HUGE difference when you are dealing with many projects at a time and when you need to dig into your archives from years ago to find a specific file. It would take very little effort for me to find a cue from a film I scored in 2016, thanks to this system.

Composers are Entrepreneurs

Composers are entrepreneurs too. Like Michael Gerber explains in his book *The E Myth Revisited*, if you don't treat your composing career like any other business, it would likely fail in 3 years.

Use a Customer Relationship Management (CRM) tool to cold email your potential prospects, asking them how you could add value to their projects with your service and follow-up when you don't hear back from them. Steli Efti, CEO of Close.io, suggests that you could use a simple follow-up cycle:

- Day 1: introductory email
- Day 3: 1st follow-up
- Day 7: 2nd follow-up
- Day 14: 3rd follow-up
- Day 28: 4th follow-up
- Day 58: 5th follow-up
- After Day 58: follow-up once a month

Understand that it takes time to work on your people skills to build relationships. If you are emailing CEOs, then follow-up only once a month. That's how you build a relationship with strangers. Also, use

PayPal for invoicing or sending estimates; they only charge when there is a transaction.

The Importance of Showreel & Credits

In order to gain the trust of an accomplished studio, franchise, producer, or a director, you must have a good body of work, exhibiting both your music skills and your ability to become a brand. The Tamil film *Roja* released in 1992, and within a short span of time, its soundtrack album sales soared. It is composer AR Rahman's first movie project, but he created a brand for himself with the score, which finds a place in the list of 10 Best Soundtracks in *Time Magazine*. The film industry trusted him and his brand, and though he was too young in the music scene, he was subsequently hired for other major movie projects, leading to the Oscar. So in order for someone to risk their project and hire you as a composer, you must be able to give an incredible emotional experience to your audience and also have enough good credits to back you as a brand.

Of course, this takes its own sweet time, but when it does happen, outstanding projects will find their way to you easily.

Do Not Update Your Software

Don't blow up your budget on buying a new gear after receiving the upfront fee for any project. And never update your software when you are in between scoring a project. It may result in your machine crashing for unknown reasons, unfixed new bugs, etc. So keep your template ready and have the gears figured out before you start any project.

Always Meet the Deadlines

The worst thing that you can do to ruin your career is not meet your deadlines. Block your calendar and work in reverse order. It's okay to use presets and mix and match it with other instruments, especially when you don't have time to redesign any sound. This is where templates come in handy. In the TV or Ad film campaign world, the turnaround time for music is less than 24 hours. This has led to the exponential growth of both sample libraries and templates.

Develop your own organised efficient workflow and never miss the deadline, for people in the industry will not forgive you if you miss it.

Have a Folder Structure

To stay organized, before I start any project, I group all the project related files into their respective categories.

Movies folder – all reels from the production studio

Transfers folder – all stems from the production studio

First Sketches folder – I have two templates for film scoring, one in Cubase and another in Logic Pro; initial sketching created from the chosen template is stored in this folder

Cues folder – from the sketches, I develop fully layered cues and save each cue as a separate project in this folder

Assemblies folder - all exports for previews and approvals are saved here

THE COMPOSER'S ASSISTANT'S HANDBOOK

- ▼ FILMSCORING - FILE_ORG
  - ▼ _00 - MOVIES
    - ▶ _00_01_LOCKED PICTURE
    - ▶ _00_02_UNLOCKED PICTURE
    - ▶ _00_03_COMPRESSED PICTURE
  - ▼ _01 - TRANSFERS
    - ▶ _01_01_DIALOGUES
    - ▶ _01_02_SFX
    - ▶ _01_03_TEMP MUSIC
  - ▼ _02 - CUE SHEETS
    - ▶ _02_01_INTIAL
    - ▶ _02_02_SECOND DRAFT
    - ▶ _02_03_FINAL
  - ▼ _03 - FIRST SKETCHES
    - ▶ _CB
    - ▶ _LPX
  - ▼ _04 - CUES
    - ▶ _04_01_INTIAL
    - ▶ _04_02_SECOND DRAFT
    - ▶ _04_03_FINAL
  - ▼ _05 - ASSEMBLIES
    - ▶ _05_01_CLIPS_MP4
    - ▶ _05_02_MP3
    - ▶ _05_03_WAV
    - ▶ _05_04_FOR_PREVIEW
    - ▶ _05_05_WAV INTERNAL
  - ▼ _06 - SHEET MUSIC
  - ▼ _07 - RECORDINGS
    - ▶ _07_01_VOCALS
    - ▶ _07_02_INSTRUMENTS
  - ▼ _08 - MIDI
  - ▼ _09 - TO THE DUBSTAGE
    - ▶ 09_01_WAV STEREO STEMS
    - ▶ 09_02_WAV STEREO MIX
    - ▶ 09_03_WAV STEREO MASTER
    - ▶ 09_04_WAV 5.1 MIX
    - ▶ 09_05_WAV 5.1 MASTER
  - ▼ _10 - PT MUSIC MIX
    - ▶ _10_01_INTIAL
    - ▶ _10_02_SECOND
    - ▶ _10_03_FINAL

Back-up

Always back-up whatever you are working on and then back-up that backup.

Using the tool Carbon Copy Cloner, I always have 3 backups – 2 offline on 2 separate HDDs and 1 on cloud. I use Google Drive for cloud because it uploads the data faster.

Self-love

Music is all about love and creating musical memories. Once, I asked composer Santhosh Narayanan how he creates such beautiful melodies. He replied, 'from my life experiences.' Yes, whoever YOU have been since your childhood will reflect in your music. So it's important that you seek help from books and professionals and heal your childhood trauma, if you have any. Because, in the end, it is all about creating and spreading good energy.

Self-doubt

As artists, we tend to compare our work with that of the others and most often carry the self-doubt: am I good enough? In an interview, Ira Glass talks about this and I pretty much agree with him.

I've summarised what he says on this: 'Nobody tells people who are beginners – and I really wish somebody had told this to me – that all of us who do creative work…we get into it because we have good taste. But it's like there's a gap that for the first couple years that you're making stuff, what you're making isn't so good or great. It's trying to be good, it has ambition to be good, but it's not quite that good. But your taste – the thing that got you into the game – your taste is still killer, and your taste is good enough that you can tell that what you're making is kind of a disappointment to you, you know what I mean? A lot of people never get past that phase. A lot of people at that point, they quit. And the thing I would like to say to you with all my heart is that most everybody I know who does interesting creative work have gone through a phase of years where they had really good taste and they could tell what they were making wasn't as good as they wanted it to be; they knew it fell short; it didn't have the special thing that we wanted it to have. Everybody goes through that. And if you are going through it right now or if you are just getting out of that phase – you gotta know that it's totally normal. And the most important thing you can do is do a huge volume of work. Put yourself on a deadline so that every week, or every month, you know you're going to finish one story. Because it's only by actually going through a volume of work that you are going to catch up and close that gap. And the work you're making will be as good as your ambitions. It takes a while and it's normal to take a while. And you just have to fight your way through that, okay?'

Fear of Missing Out (FOMO)

If you are constantly checking your phone or scrolling through your WhatsApp every 5 mins, then you might have the FOMO. This prevents you from achieving your goals. To overcome FOMO, you could try blocking 4 hours every morning for composing and the next 4 hours for replying to your emails, engaging your audience on social media, watching Netflix, etc. You could turn off notifications from social media on your computer with LeechBlock browser extension and keep your phone in aeroplane mode for 4 hours at least. Don't let the FOMO keep you from enjoying your present moment!

Have a Plan and Stick to It

Have a bird's eye view of what you want to do in media composition. Put your heart and soul and niche down to one thing — library music or game composition or composing for Film or TV. If you are good at creating 30 seconders for ad film campaigns, it does not necessarily mean that you could score a video game. And success in one field does not mean that it would lead to success in the other related fields too. So be a master of ONE thing rather than being a jack of all trades.

Nobody Owes You Anything

Like Junkie XL says, just because you spent years owning the media composition craft doesn't mean that Hollywood owes you your success. Just because you saved a director by scoring his film and scoring it well at the last minute doesn't mean he'll have to hire you in all his future projects. Nobody owes you anything! Remembering this would save you from a lot of disheartenment in the future.

Feedback

Finally, take feedback constructively rather than reacting to it. When someone says something about your work, analyse if there's any truth to it and if you feel there is, then work on it to improve; otherwise, just ignore it. It is easier said than done. It is normal to feel depressed during such times; have some drinks with your friends or get out of your studio and distract yourself by going to a movie. Then after a few days, start over fresh from the client's perspective. Try to understand why he rejected that cue/piece; then send the client the new piece. Lot of people don't do this; they get hurt and stop working on it. It's a trap! Trust me…following up with the client will definitely bring more projects to you in surprising ways!

'Inside you there's an artist you don't know about.'

~ Rumi

Throughout my life, I've always followed my heart. Pursuing music technology has not only enabled me to write good music, but it has also brought out the entrepreneur in me. In this journey of becoming and being a composer, even though I had been clueless to the obstacles and the financial ups and downs, which were unpleasant to say the least, I've also had my share of moments that have touched, moved, inspired, and healed my soul. When I look back at the journey, it has simply been amazing so far. And I'm so looking forward to all that is to come!

I would like to thank you for purchasing this book.

If you have any specific questions, suggestions, or feedback, please feel free to reach me at:

jaikumarsivalingam@pssoundspace.in

{Or}

Connect with me on:

Twitter - @jaikumarsmusic

Facebook
https://www.facebook.com/jaikumar.sivalingam

Instagram
https://www.instagram.com/jaikumarsivalingam

Cheers,

Jaikumar

Chapter 7

Tools & Resources

Be it music or any art form, I have always been fascinated by how people adds so much value for free to the crowd following them. Upon maximum utilisation, these tools, apps, and plugins have and continue to help me a lot. So I'd love to give a huge shout out to them! Hope they bring more value to you too.

Apps & Tools

SimpleMind, Mindnode – mind map tool for ideas

Quicktime player, OBS – screen recorder

MIDI monitor – tests the incoming MIDI messages to your computer

Dropbox and Box – cloud storage

Flux – adjust brightness of your computer screen

Spectacle – resizing several softwares in one screen

Close.io – most effective crm for cold calling

Video Slave 3 – host videos on a separate machine to free up RAM

Memory Diag – frees up unused RAM in your computer

Google docs, sheets, slides, calendar – store your ideas in cloud

Evernote – store everything possible here

Carbon Copy Cloner – simple efficient backup tool

TransferWise – to receive payment from international clients

PayPal – send estimates and invoices for free

Bounce Butler – saves time by batch exporting your bounces and stems

Plugins

xferOTT – It is a free re– creation of a popular multiband upwards/downwards compressor

Izotope's Ozone Imager – This free Ozone Imager plug– in can adjust stereo image with simple controls, stunning visuals, and incredible sound

iZotope Vinyl – It is perfect for music production and audio post; with Vinyl, you can control each element independently and get vintage sounds

iZotope Vocal Doubler – It is a free plug– in designed to enhance your vocal with a natural doubling effect, adding richness and depth

Voxengo SPAN – SPAN is a spectrum analyzer that displays level metering statistics

Polyverse Wider – Wider is a stereo plugin that is completely mono– compatible

Flux Bittersweet – It is a transient processor used for audio transient management with the simple turn of a knob

Cableguys PanCake – PanCake is used for creating panning modulations

Softube Saturation Knob – Saturation Knob is a modeled output distortion that can be used to fatten up bass lines, add some harmonics and shimmer to vocals, or simply destroy the drum loop

Free Virtual Instruments

Orchestral Tools – Layers – Free Orchestral Library. Captured at Teldex Scoring Stage in Berlin

Spitfire Audio LABS – It is an infinite series of software instruments

Project SAM's The Free Orchestra – The Free Orchestra offers cinematic sounds taken directly from ProjectSAM's acclaimed libraries, ranging from orchestral string staccatos and brass clusters to symphonic percussion and dystopian sound design

Freelance Work

Fiverr.com

Books

Here's a list of books that have helped me immensely. Remember I told you earlier that composers are also entrepreneurs? Treating your composing career like a start–up involves a lot of self study on how a business succeeds or fails which no technical books on music could teach you. Many composers fail to obtain education to make smart decisions about the business – don't be that composer! I did not have the habit of reading books for the first 30 years of my life! But one of my mentors asked me to read just one book: *The E– Myth Revisited*. From that book, I discovered what goes into creating a successful business start-up. Understanding the intricacies, one book led me to another, and the list is ever growing.

The One Thing – Gary Keller

Anything You Want – Derek Sivers

The 5 Second Rule – Mel Robbins

The E-Myth Revisited – Michael E. Gerber

The Go-Giver – Bob Burg

The 4-Hour Work Week – Timothy Ferriss

Getting Things Done – David Allen

The Quick and Easy Way to Effective Speaking – Dale Carnegie

How to Win Friends and Influence People – Dale Carnegie

Think and Grow Rich – Napoleon Hill

The Power of your Subconscious Mind – Joseph Murphy

How to Talk to Anyone – Leil Lowndes

The $100 Startup – Chris Guillebeau

<u>Building a Story Brand</u> – Donald Miller

<u>The Compound Effect</u> – Darren Hardy

Forums

<u>Vi– control.net</u> – a place where people could speak freely about composing and sample libraries

<u>Pianobook</u> – a collective sample project inspiring musicians to embrace the magic of sampling and share their creations with the community

Facebook Groups

Perspective: A forum for film, TV, and media composers

A Composer's Guide to Library Music Discussion

Chapter 8

Acknowledgements

Thank you.

AR Rahman and Hans Zimmer for inspiring me and helping me learn so much through your music, interviews, and masterclass. I wouldn't be doing what I love if your music had not ruffled ever so gently my emotions.

Thank you Lesle Lewis – Singer, Songwriter, and Composer; Adrushta Deepak Pallikonda – Grammy Winning Mix Engineer; Pradeep Kumar Vijay – Singer, Songwriter, and Composer; Radhan – Songwriter and Composer; Arijit Datta – Singer, Songwriter, and Composer for giving me the opportunity to be an intern/ composer assistant and learn your process and workflow.

My Dad, who always told me to get out of my comfort zone and move to a place where there are people who do what I wanted to do.

My Mom for teaching me to read the treble clef and bass clef. I'm glad that it just didn't stop there!

Hentry Kuruvila for not just being a teacher but also a great mentor and a good friend!

Thanks, Praveen, for being very supportive throughout my ups and downs!

Thanks to my loving wife for making me believe in myself and my music. And for helping me to write this book.

I would also like to thank:

Aashish Rego, Abe Thomas, Aditi Padiyar, Aditya Modi, Aditya Pushkarna, Ahrai Washington, Akash Thakkar, Akshay Sreeram, Alex Moukala, Alex Pfeffer, Alok Punjani, Alokananda Dasgupta, Alyssa Menes, Andy Hill,, Anisha Peter, Appu Krishnan, Arjun Janakiram, Arn Anderson, Ashton Gleckman, Aum Janakiram, Ben Newhouse, Bethel Tsuzu, Bill Burgess, Bill Piyatut H, Bishwadeep Dipak Chatterjee, Blake Robinson, Bobby Owsinski, Brian Hood, Chance Thomas, Charlie Clouser, Chris Graham, Christian Henson, Cody Still, Dan Graham, Daniel Beijbom, Daniel Ciurlizza, Daniel

James, Darius Moldovan, David Earl, David Fleming, Deepak Bhojraj, Devdatta Waghmare, Dinesh Sivaraj, Eli Krantzberg, Erik Aho, Farhad K Dadyburjor, Francis Perry, Ganesh K Raju, Geetha Ramesh Iyengar, Geoff Manchester, Germaine Franco, Goran Dragaš, Graham Cochrane, Gunjan Pancholi, Guy Michelmore, Noam Levy, Hari Baskar, Harikrishnan R, Harry Gregson Williams, Harshavardhan Rameshwar, Homay Schmitz, Ira Glass, Jacob Shea, Jacob Yoffee, James Newton Howard, Jason Graves, Jason Zachariah, Jay Swaminathan, Jecin George, Jeremiah John, Jim Satya, Joël Dollié, Joel Dsouza, John Paesano, John Powell, John Stewart Eduri, Joshua Carney, Joy Banerjee, Julia Lorenz Olson, Junkie XL, K J Singh, Kanna Ravi, Kashyap Iyengar, Kaveh Cohen, Kristopher Carter, Lewis Pravin, Lillian Zachariah, Manoj Kumar, Marc D Muse, Mary Joseph, Meghdeep Bose, Michael Mass, Mirela Magdalena Nita, Mohamaad Ghibran, Mohammed Rizwan, Mohit Kachalia, Nakash Aziz, Narayanan S P, Nariman Khambata, Nima Fakhara, Nitish R Kumar, Oliver Patrice Weder, Padmapriya Narayanan, Paul Haslinger, Paul Rodney J, Paul

Thomson, Penka D Kouneva, Peter Schwartz, Phil Lober, Philip Olson, Pinar Toprak, Prashan Jayatheepan, Pravin Mani, Radhan, Rahul Pais, Rahul Ram Chandran, Rain Ventsel, Raju Singh Panesar, Reena Gilbert, Richard Kraft, Rick Beato, Rolfe Kent, Rupert Gregson Williams, Russ Hughes, Ryan Leach, Santhosh Narayanan, Sean Roldan, Sethu Thankachan, Shadab Rayeen, Sharanya Natrajan, Sharmi Chakraborty, Sourav Roy, Steli Efti, Sudha Swaminathan, Sunny M R, Tanuj Tiku, Thomas Newman, Tristan Noon, Vairavasan Alagappan, Veenaa Bhakshi, Vijay Rathinam, Vikas Rawat, Vivek Mano, Walid Feghali, Wilson Kenneth, Winifred Phillips, Yasha Pandit.

www.ingramcontent.com/pod-product-compliance
Lightning Source LLC
Chambersburg PA
CBHW050254220526
45465CB00002B/676